Mel Bay Presents

CHORDS GALORE

A Systematic Approach to Voicing Chords on Guitar

by Jack Petersen

2 3 4 5 6 7 8 9 0

Visit us on the Web at www.melbay.com — E-mail us at email@melbay.com

Table of Contents

Foreword

This book is designed for young and old students to gain a better understanding of chord construction and voice them on the guitar fingerboard. This book deals with four note chords. However, more notes can be added to these chords on other strings wherever possible. It is expected that the student has knowledge of chord construction, standard notation, how to read tablature, and chord diagrams. Every jazz player I've seen or heard uses these chord types. Here is a list of some jazz guitarists that use the chords presented in this book:

Johnny Smith	Tal Farlow
Jimmy Rainey	George Benson
Russell Malone	Oscar Moore
Herb Ellis	Joe Pass
Pat Metheny	Antonio Carlos Jobim
Luis Bonfa	Howard Alden
Jack Wilkins	James Chirillo
Bucky Pizzarrelli	John Pizzarelli
Jimmy Bruno	Mike Stern
Mick Goodrick	John Abercrombie
Nathan Page	

Chapter 1

A **chord** is the sounding of three or more notes simultaneously. Chords are built from scales. Most guitar books refer to chords as **chord forms**. In this book, chords will be referred to as **chord voicings**. Chord voicings are rearrangement of the notes of a chord. Understanding how to rearrange notes within a chord is paramount for a guitarist. Chords are formed by stacking every other note in a scale.

C major scale

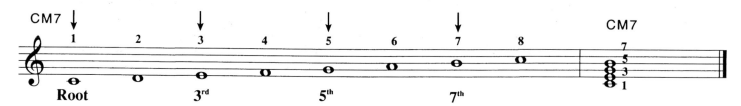

A chord can be built from any one of the notes in a scale.

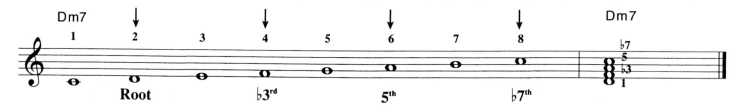

This procedure constructs G chords in close position. A chord built in close position is built with intervals of thirds. The following exercise consists of chords based from the G major scale in arpeggio form.

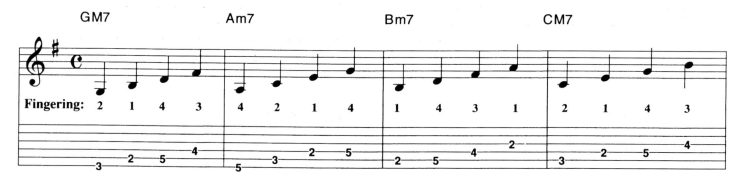

Playing these chord tones simultaneously in close position is impossible. Since the guitar is not tuned in the intervals of 3^{rds}, a different approach is necessary.

The guitar is tuned in intervals of perfect 4^{ths} with an interval of a major 3rd between the 3rd and 2nd string. There are many chord voicings in the open strings. Explanation of how to create chords from the open strings are in the next two pages.

Step 1 – Play the G Major scale on the G string or 3rd string.

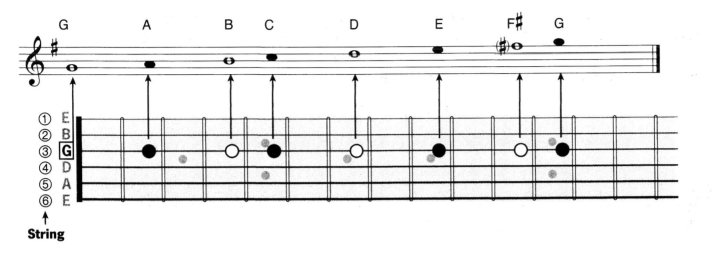

Step 2 – Add the B or 2nd string to the third string. This creates double stops or a scale built using intervals of thirds.

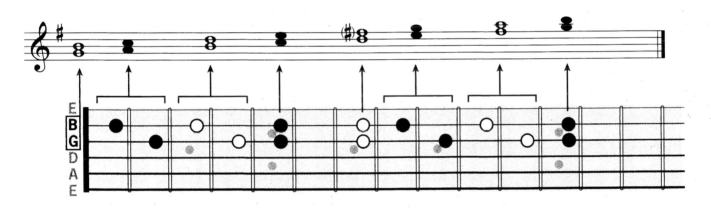

Step 3 – Add the 4th string to the 2nd and 3rd strings. This creates diatonic triads.

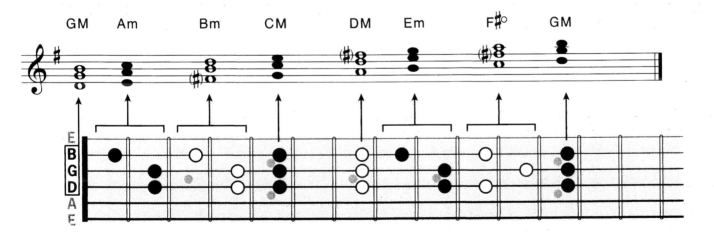

Step 4 – Add the 6th string to 2nd, 3rd, and 4th string. This creates diatonic seventh chords.

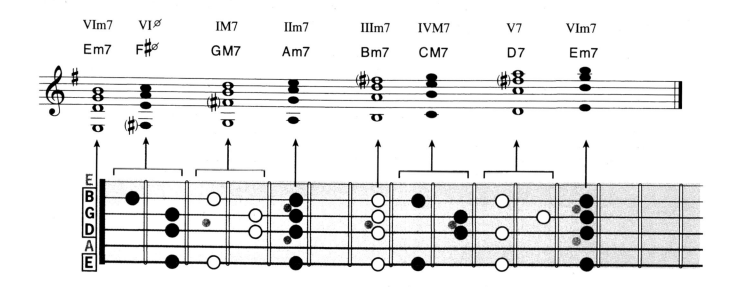

By analyzing the voices of the seventh chords, we can see the chords have been rearranged from close position. The two inner voices have been moved up one octave from the original.

◆ = Root

GM7   **(Raised 2 and 3)**

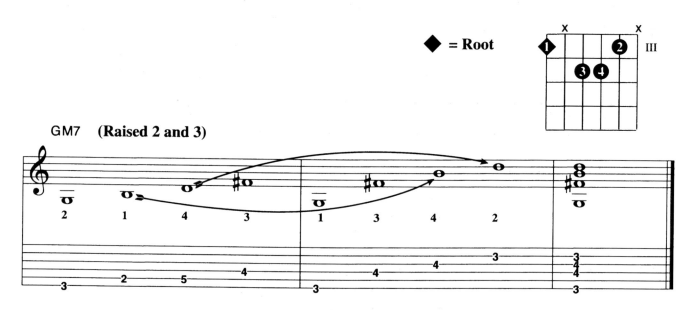

This is a good formula for voicing chords from the 6th string. This is called a **raised two and three voicing**. (R2+3) There are three steps in constructing these chords from the 6th string:

   1.– Arpeggiate the chord from the 6th string

   2.– Transpose the second and third notes of the arpeggio up one octave.

   3.– Place the notes in this manner,

- Highest note on 2nd string.

- Second highest note on 3rd string.

- Third highest note on 4th string.

- Lowest note on 6th string.

These chord construction techniques are based on the major scale. The root is the first note of a scale, root note is also the note that names a chord. The 3rd, 5th, and 7th notes of the major scale completes the major seventh chord. The following chart shows various types of seventh chords on the left. The intervals used to construct chords from the major scale are all on the right.

Major Seven	M7	Root, 3, 5, 7
Seven	7	Root, 3, 5, ♭7
Six	6	Root, 3, 5, 6
Minor Major Seven	mM7	Root, ♭3, 5, 7
Minor Seven	m7	Root, ♭3, 5, ♭7
Minor Six	m6	Root, ♭3, 5, 6
Major Seven Sharp Five	M7(+5)	Root, 3, +5, 7
Major Seven Flat Five	M7(♭5)	Root, 3, ♭5, 7
Seven Sharp Five	7(+5)	Root, 3, +5, ♭7
Seven Flat Five	7(♭5)	Root, 3, ♭5, ♭7
Minor Seven Sharp Five	m7(+5)	Root, ♭3, +5, ♭7
Minor Seven Flat Five	m7(♭5)	Root, ♭3, ♭5, ♭7
(Same as Half Diminished)	∅	Root, ♭3, ♭5, ♭7
Diminished	°	Root, ♭3, ♭5, ♭♭7(6)
Sus Four	sus4	Root, 4, 5, 7

The difference between major seven and seven is one note:

$$M7 \quad = \quad \textbf{Root, 3, 5, 7}$$
$$7 \quad = \quad \textbf{Root, 3, 5, ♭7} \quad \text{(1/2 step)}$$

The difference between a seventh and a major sixth chord is one note:

$$7 \quad = \quad \textbf{Root, 3, 5, ♭7} \quad \text{(1/2 step)}$$
$$6 \quad = \quad \textbf{Root, 3, 5, 6}$$

The root, 3rd, and 5th on all three chords are the same. The major 7th is altered.

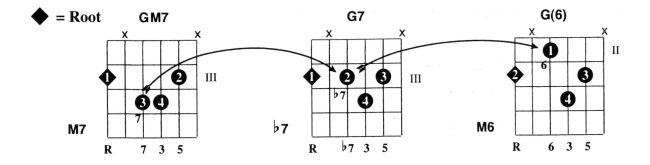

7

Placement of the root, 3rd and 5th remain in the same fret, but the fingering changes. the same procedure can be used for minor chords. The difference between minor major seven and minor seven is one note:

$$\text{mM7} \quad = \quad \text{Root, } \flat 3, 5, 7$$
$$\text{m7} \quad = \quad \text{Root, } \flat 3, 5, \flat 7 \qquad \text{(1/2 step)}$$

The difference between minor seven and minor six is one note:

$$\text{m7} \quad = \quad \text{Root, } \flat 3, 5, \flat 7$$
$$\text{m6} \quad = \quad \text{Root, } \flat 3, 5, 6 \qquad \text{(1/2 step)}$$

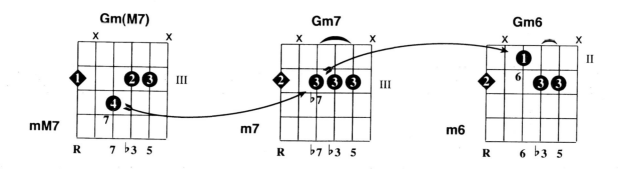

Learning to use these voicings is a very simple process. When the chord symbol is CM7, find the note C on the 6th string and build the major seven raised 2 and 3 voicing from the note. The following page consists of a chord progression using only raised 2 and 3 voicings.

Chord Ex. 1

Six chord types are used in this chord progression! (The major seven, seven, major sixth, minor major seven, minor seven, and minor six chords.)

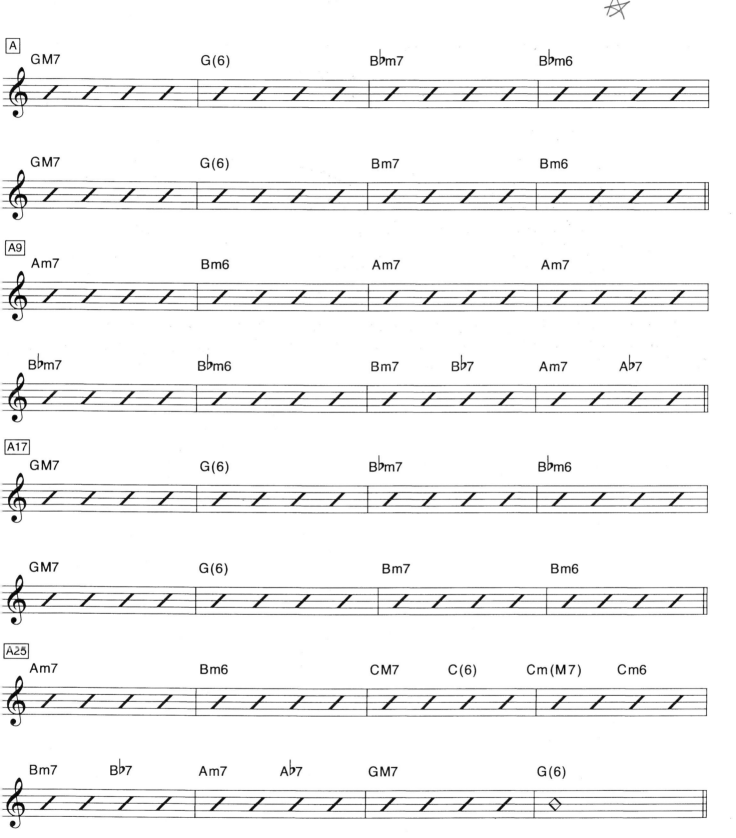

Six chord types were used in this chord progression!

Seven Flat Five Chords

To create 7♭5 or 7♯5 chord, simply move the 5th of the chord up or down one fret.

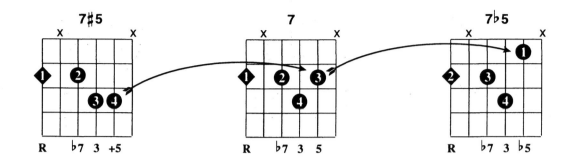

The following progression contains four-note chords with the lowest note on the 6th string.

Chord Ex. 2

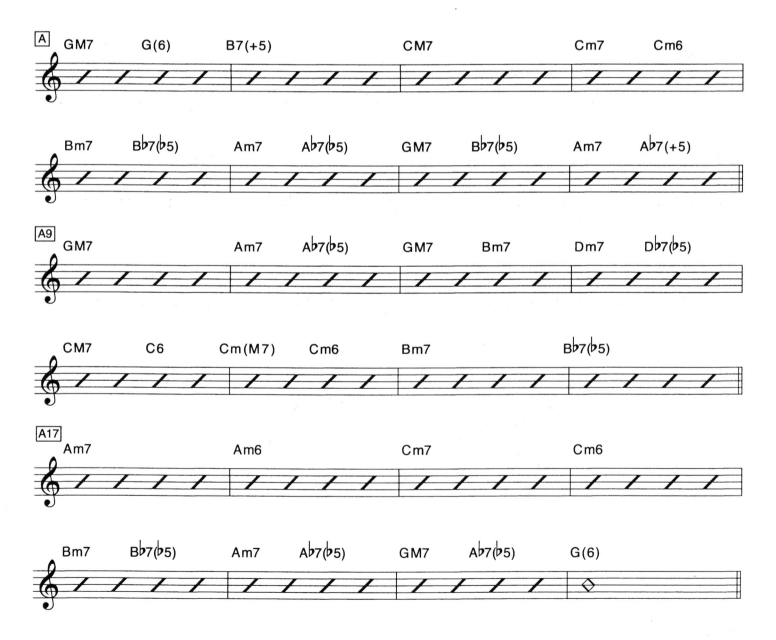

Altering the 5th of a minor seven chord can help create interesting chord progressions. Minor seven flat five and half diminished chords are the same chord.

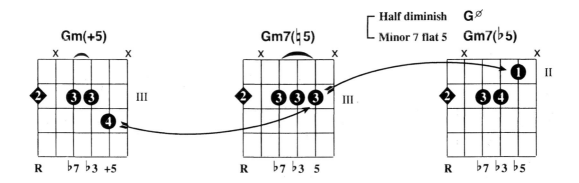

The following chord progression contains these chord voicings.

Chord Ex. 3

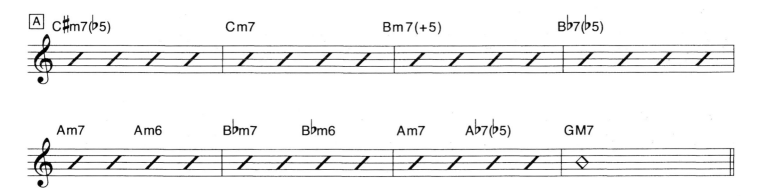

A diminished chord consists of root, flat 3rd, flat 5th, and diminished (double flat)7th. A double flat 7th is the same as the 6th (root, b3, b5, and 6). By flating the 3rd and 5th of a major six chord, this creates a diminished chord.

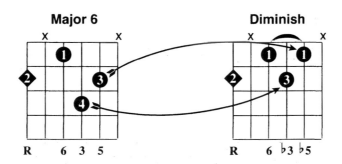

The symbol for a diminished seventh chord is a circle. (C°7). The symbol for a half diminished has a slash through the circle C∅. Another type of diminished chord is diminished major seven chord C°(M7).

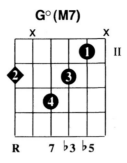

G°(M7)

R　7　♭3　♭5

Chord Ex. 4

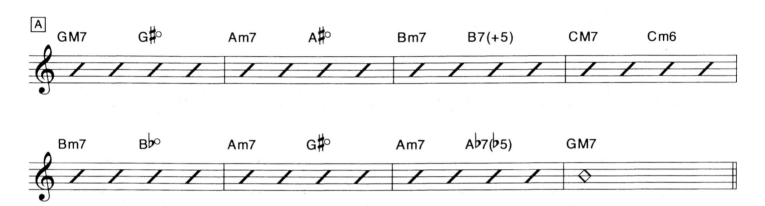

| GM7 | G♯° | Am7 | A♯° | Bm7 | B7(+5) | CM7 | Cm6 |

| Bm7 | B♭° | Am7 | G♯° | Am7 | A♭7(♭5) | GM7 |

Not all chords are based from root position. A **root position chord** is a chord with the root as the lowest tone. **Inversions** are chords that have different notes in the bass other than the root. Another description for a chord inversion is permutation. A simple numerical permutation is to move the first number in a set over to the right to create a new set of numbers.

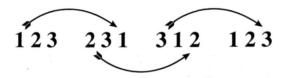

1 2 3　　2 3 1　　3 1 2　　1 2 3

Doing this to a triad will create inversions

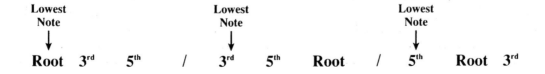

| Lowest Note ↓ | | | | Lowest Note ↓ | | | | Lowest Note ↓ | |
| Root | 3rd | 5th | / | 3rd | 5th | Root | / | 5th | Root | 3rd |

Inverting triads can be done on the guitar. To invert a triad, take the bottom note and move it one octave higher.

12

C Major Triad with Inversions

When inverting four-note chords (seventh chords), simply moving the lowest note up an octave to create inversions does not work out easily on the guitar. A different approach must be used. Start with the E minor seven chord using the open strings (E,B,G,D).

Step 1 – Play an E minor seven arpeggio on the 2nd or B string

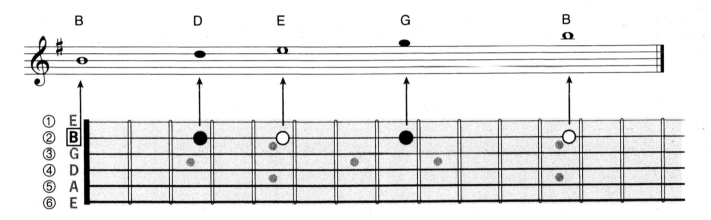

Step 2 – Add the chord tones on the 3rd or G string.

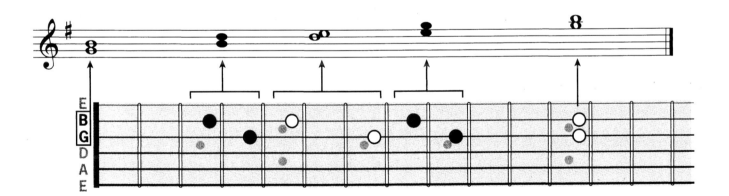

13

Step 3 – Add the chord tones on the 4th or D string.

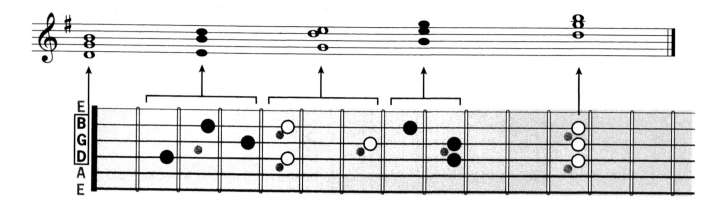

Step 4 – Add the chord tones on the 6th or E string.

This approach is horizontal.

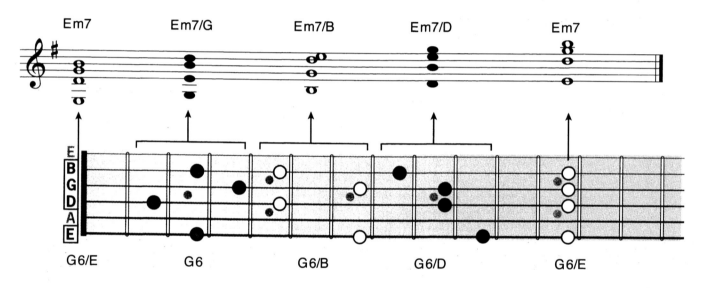

Notice this chord has two different names, Em7 and G6 are enharmonic chords. They have the same notes, but not the same function.

Chord inversions:

- Root is in bass = root position
- 3rd is in bass = first inversion
- 5th is in bass = second inversion
- 6th or 7th is in bass = third inversion.

By analyzing the voicings of the inversions, the same formula applies to inversions, raise 2 and 3 (**R2+3**)

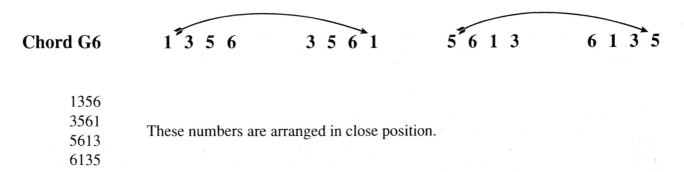

Chord G6   1 3 5 6   3 5 6 1   5 6 1 3   6 1 3 5

1356
3561
5613
6135

These numbers are arranged in close position.

Take the two inner numbers and move them to the right of the numerical sequence.

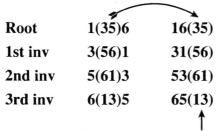

Root	1(35)6	16(35)
1st inv	3(56)1	31(56)
2nd inv	5(61)3	53(61)
3rd inv	6(13)5	65(13)

↑

This creates raised 2+3 voicing for each inversion.

The following examples show how to build inversions for a G6 chord. Memorize the chord patterns but also memorize the chord construction process.

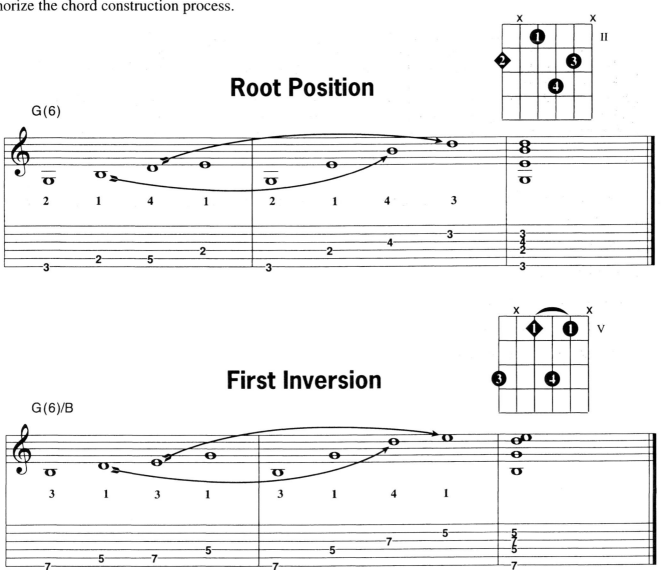

Root Position

G(6)

First Inversion

G(6)/B

Second Inversion

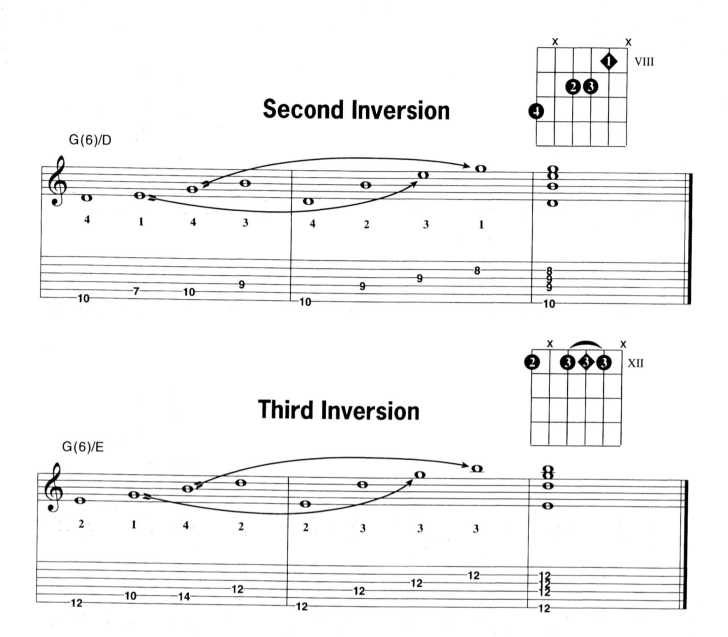

Third Inversion

When examining a chord progression, scan the chord sheet and find the inversions first. All the rest of the chords will be in root position. Use the formula (R2+3) when constructing inversions instead of adjusting the notes within the chord voicing.

The following chord progression has nine inversions. Some of them are repeated. Without the repeated inversions there are seven different E chord types.

Check marks indicate inverted chords

Chord Ex. 5

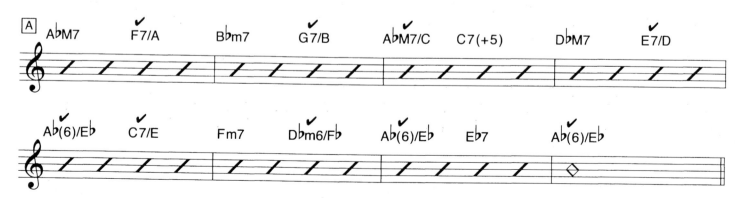

16

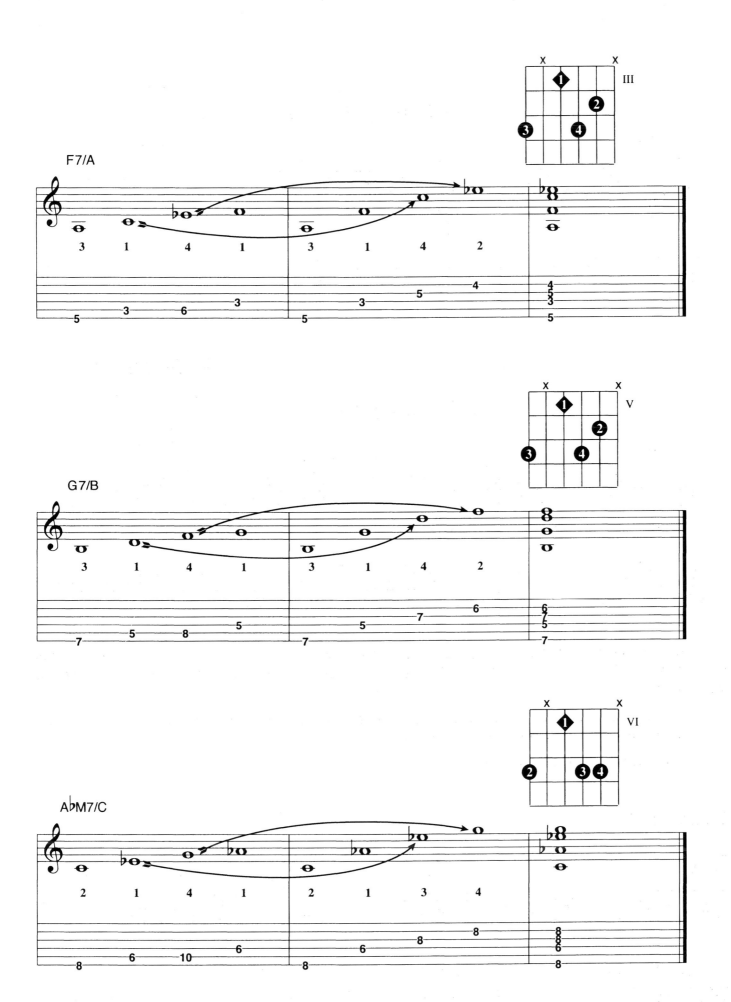

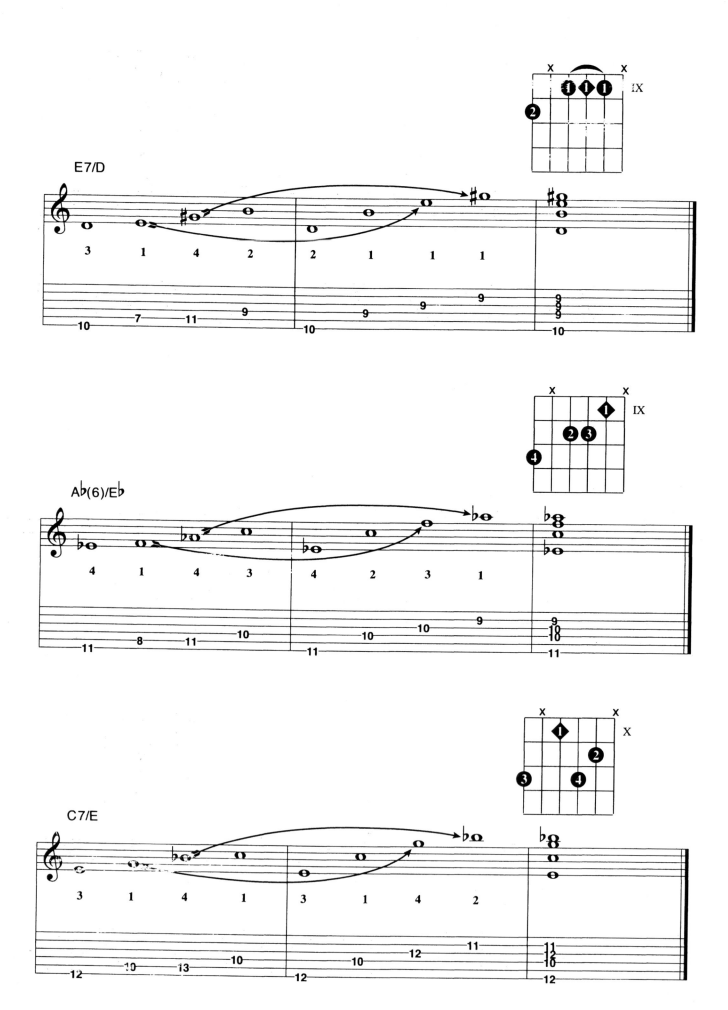

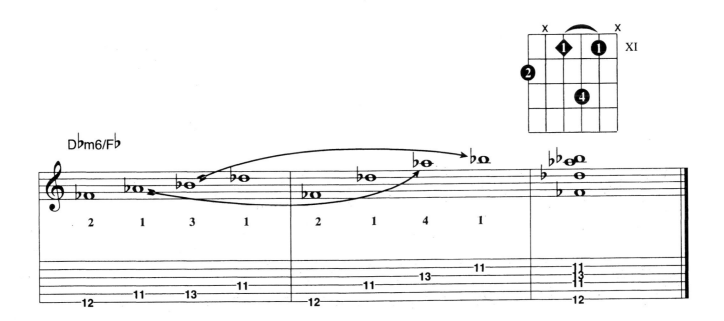

Dbm6/Fb

Chord Ex. 6

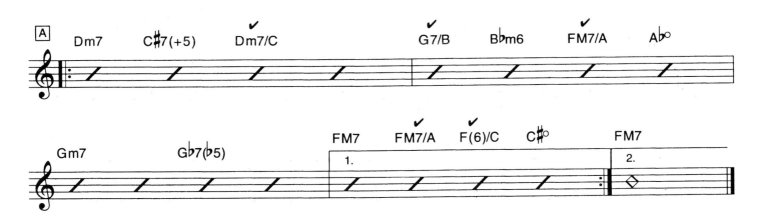

A
Dm7   C#7(+5)   Dm7/C   G7/B   Bbm6   FM7/A   Abo

Gm7   Gb7(b5)   FM7   FM7/A   F(6)/C   C#o   FM7

1.   2.

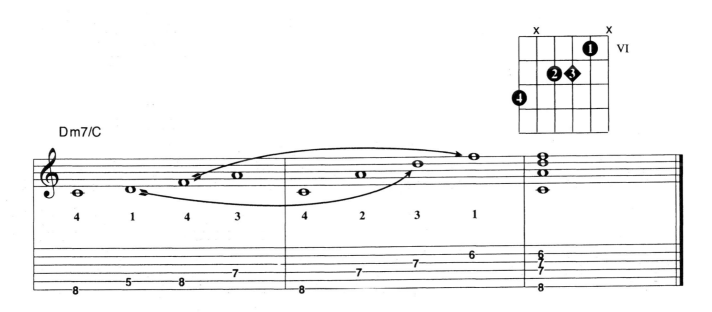

Dm7/C

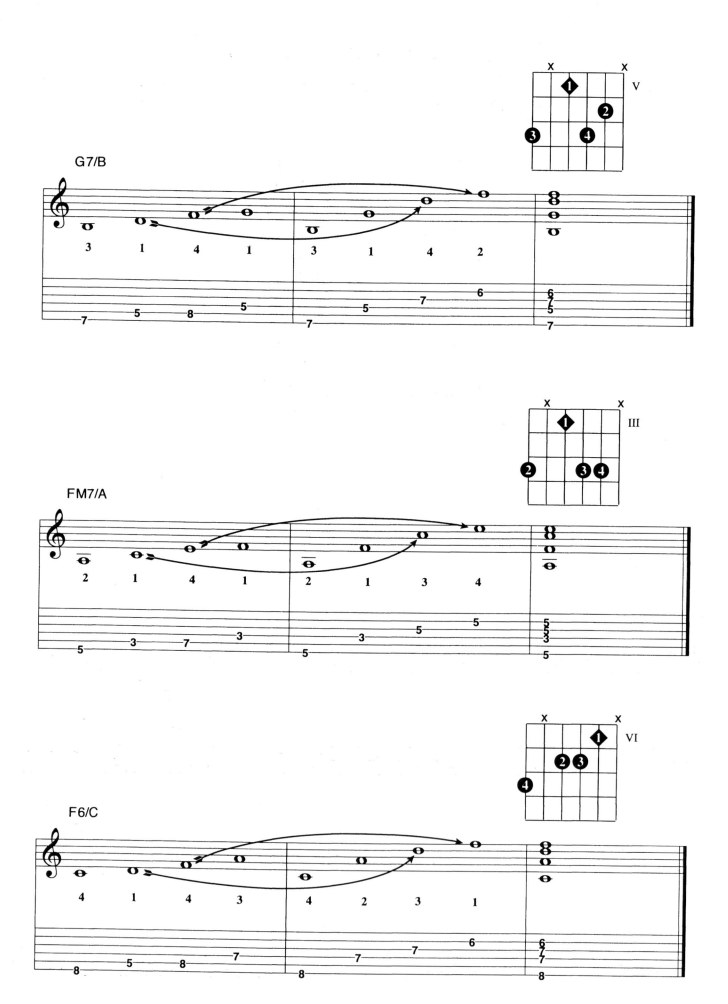

Suspended Fourth Chords (sus 4)

A good definition of sus 4 is to use the 4th degree of a major scale instead of the 3rd, even if the 3rd is major or minor. The 4th degree replaces the third degree.

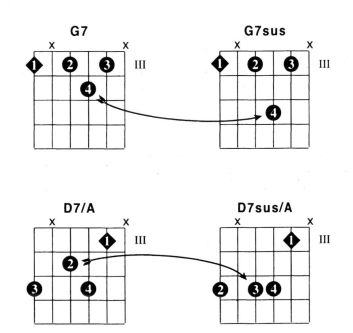

Practice the following etudes to learn suspended fourth chords.

Chord Ex7

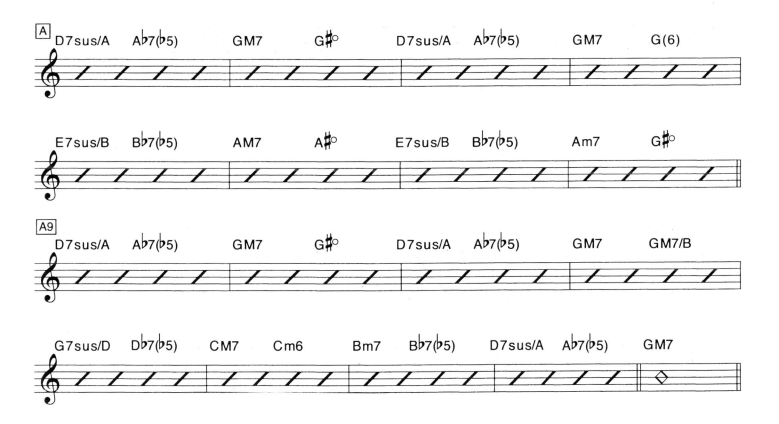

Chapter 2

Chord Voicings Based from the 5th String.

A good formula for building chords with the lowest note on the 5th string is to raise the second note of a close position arpeggio.

C M7   **(Raised 2)**

This is a good formula for voicing chords from the 5th string. This is called a **raised two voicing (R2)**. There are three steps in constructing these chords from the 5th string.

1.– Play the chord in arpeggiated form from the 5th string.

2.– Move the second note of the arpeggio up one octave.

3.– Place the notes in this order,

   • Highest note on 2nd string.
   • Second highest note on 3rd string.
   • Third highest note on 4th string.
   • Lowest note on 5th string.

This major chord is in root position. Alter the major seven to flat seven and major six. The root, 5th, and 3rd remain on the same fret, but the fingering changes.

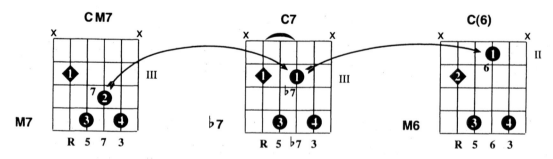

To change a major seventh chord to a minor major seventh chord, simply lower the 3rd degree. To create minor seventh and minor sixth chords, simply move the 7th degree of the minor major seventh chord down one and two frets.

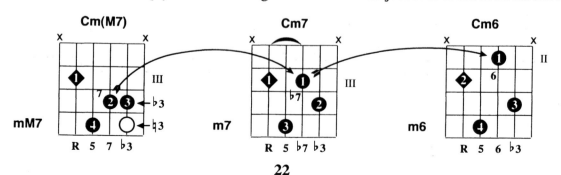

22

Learning to use these voicings can be a very simple process. When the chord symbol is Dm7, find the note D on the 5th string and build the D minor seven voicing from that fret. Repeat this process for every chord in a progression. The following exercise consists of a chord progression using all six chord types.

Chord Ex 8

Here are dominant seventh (1, 3, 5, ♭7) chords with the 5th altered.

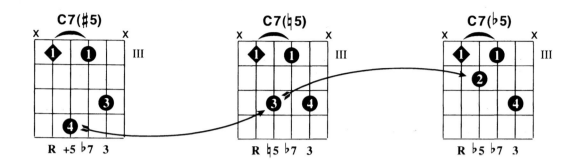

Chord Ex. 9

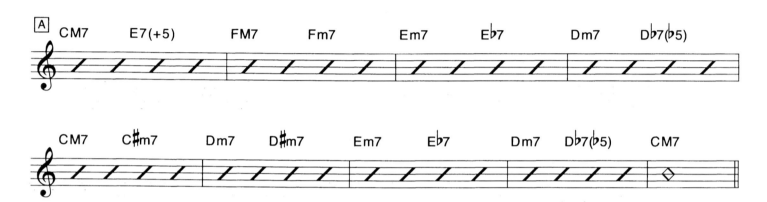

Here are minor seven chords with the 5th altered.

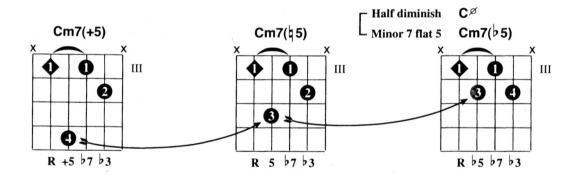

Remember: Minor seven flat five has two names. The other name is half diminished.

Chord Ex. 10

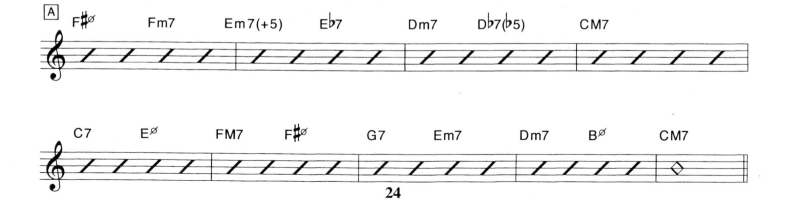

24

A diminished chord consists of flating the 3rd and 5th of a major six chord. To create a diminished major seven chord, flat the 3rd and 5th of a major seven chord.

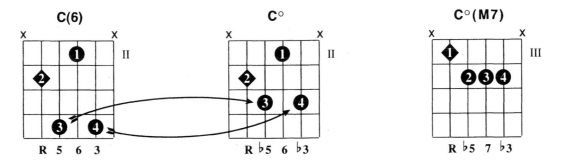

Chord Ex. 11

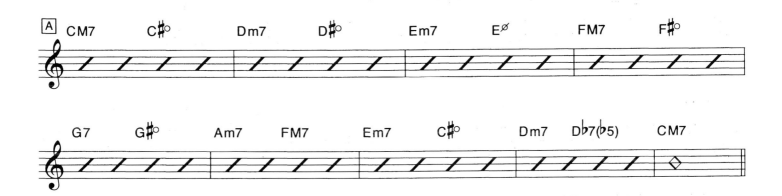

The formula for raised two (R2) voicings applies for inversions with the lowest note on the 5th string. Using the formula (R2), construct each inversion for all four-note chords (Maj7, m7, Maj6, m6, 7, °7, ∅7) and their alterations.

(Raised Two)

Root Position

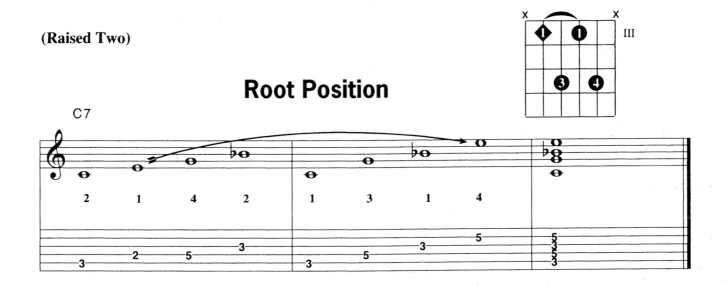

25

First Inversion

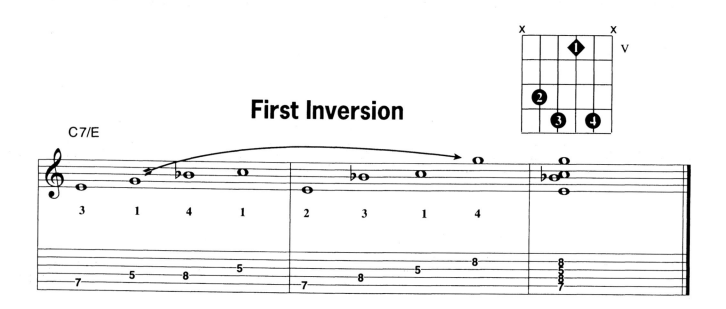

Second Inversion

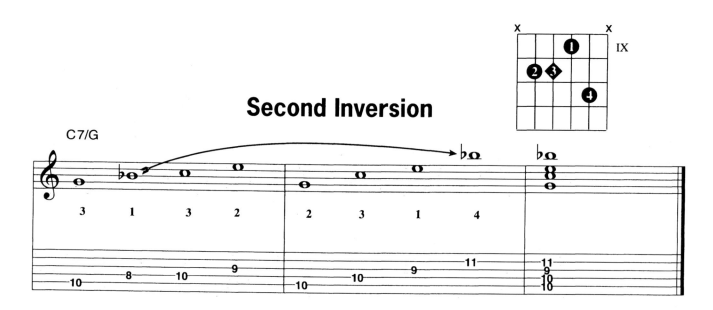

Third Inversion

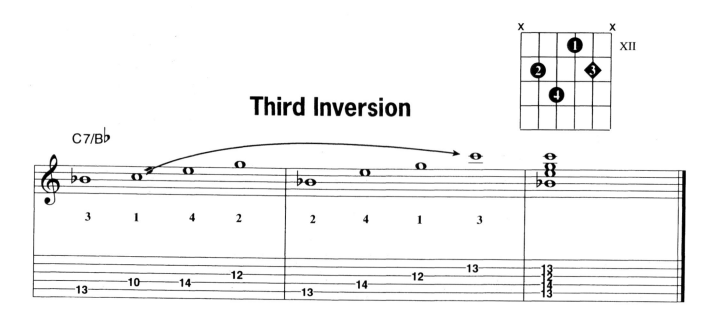

Chord Ex. 12

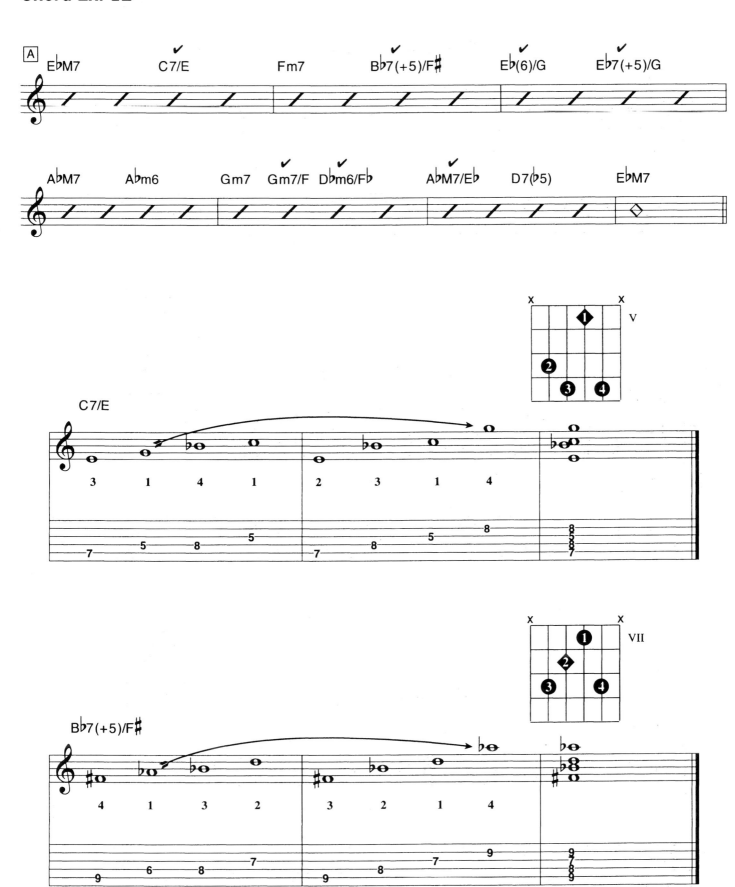

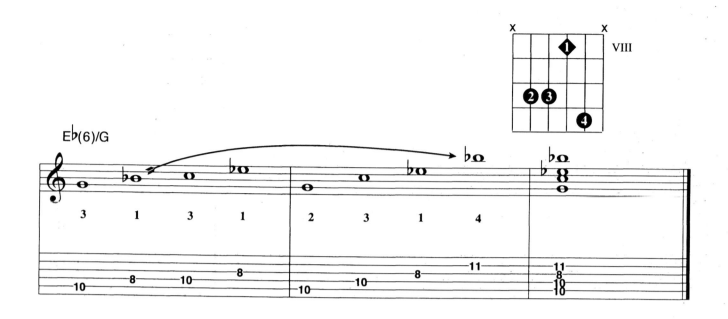

Eb(6)/G

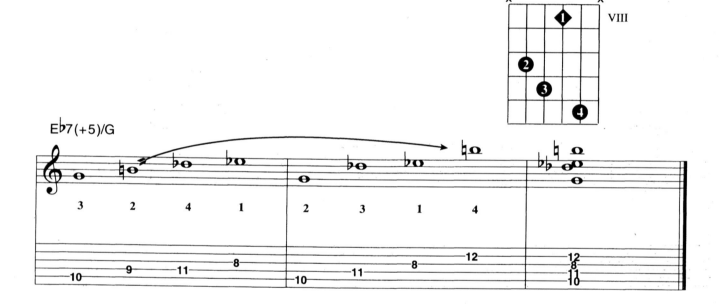

Eb7(+5)/G

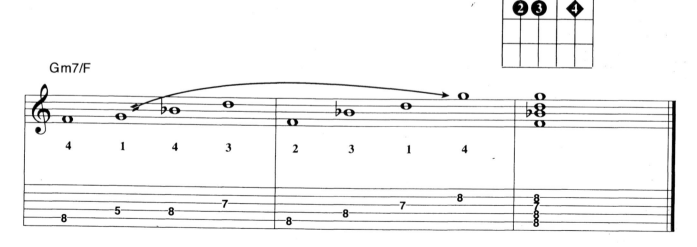

Gm7/F

28

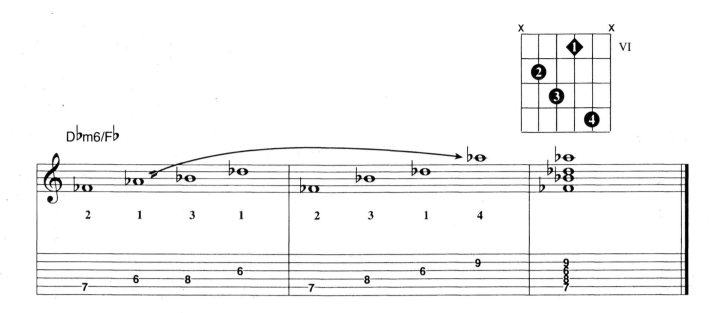

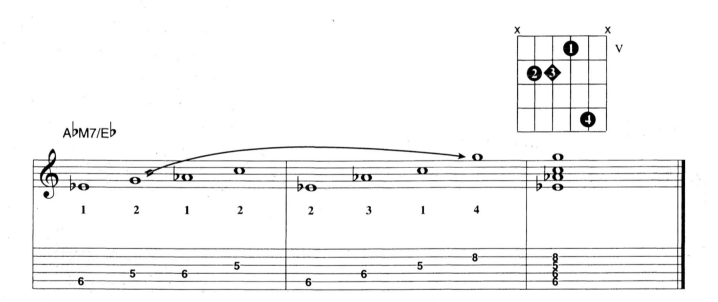

Chord Ex. 13

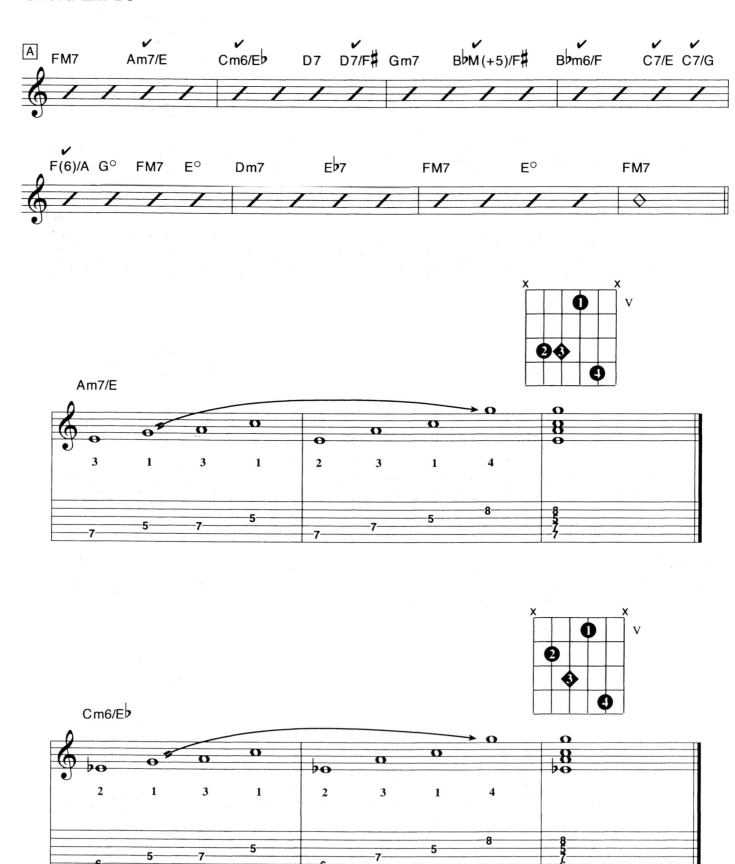

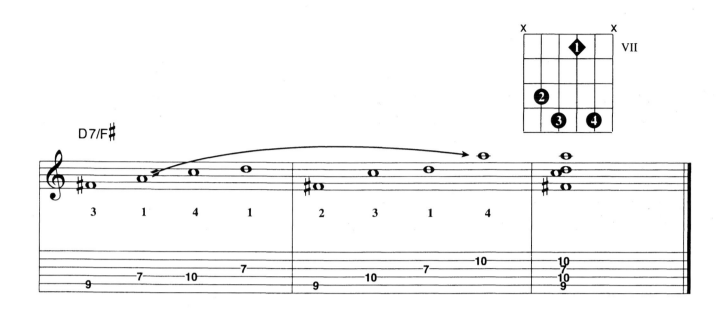

D7/F♯

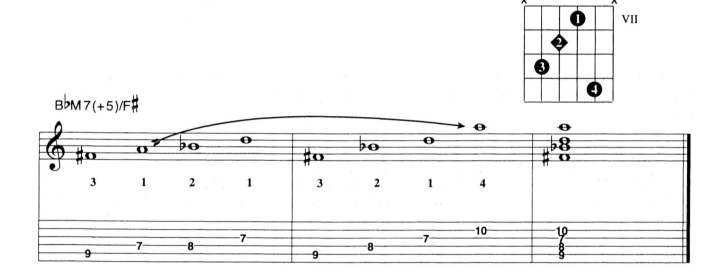

B♭M7(+5)/F♯

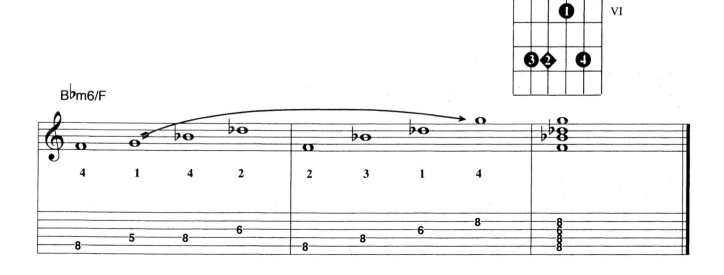

B♭m6/F

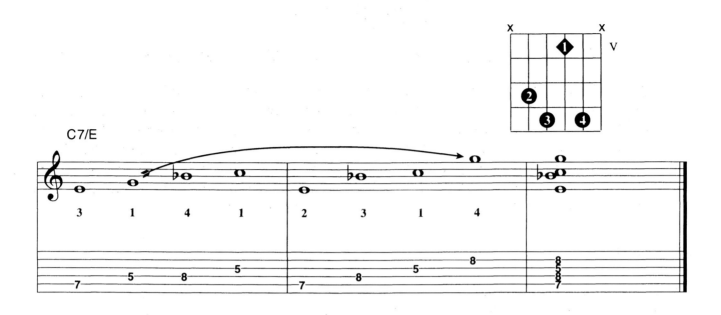

C7/E

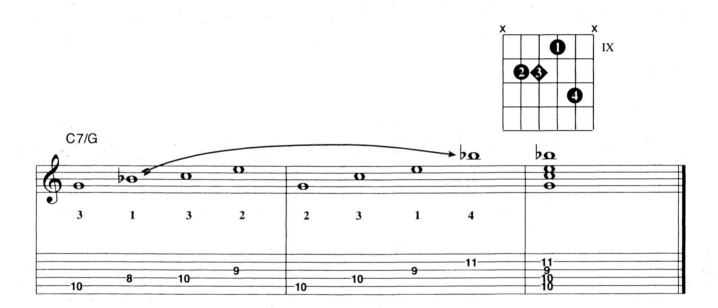

C7/G

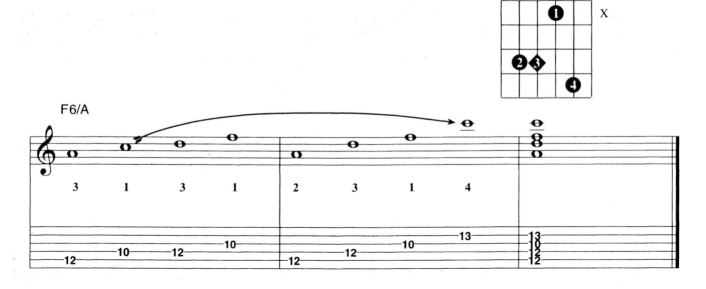

F6/A

Chapter 3

Combining and Alternating Between 5ᵗʰ and 6ᵗʰ Strings

The purpose of this concept is to create greater motion from one chord to the next. The key to understanding this concept is placement of the bass notes. Upon first observation of a chord progression, automatically look at the bass notes for each chord first, and place them either on the 5ᵗʰ or 6ᵗʰ string. For example, if a progression has C7 moving to Fm7, be concerned about the note C moving to the note F. If the note C is placed on the 6ᵗʰ string, then F is in the same fret, but on the 5ᵗʰ string. The formula (R2+3) would be used to build a C7 chord on the 6ᵗʰ string, and the formula (R2) would be used to build a Fm7 on the 5ᵗʰ string. (R2/R2+3) indicates what kind of voicing should be constructed. The circled number ⑤indicates what string the chord should be constructed from.

Chord Ex. 14

Chord Ex. 15

Chord Ex. 16

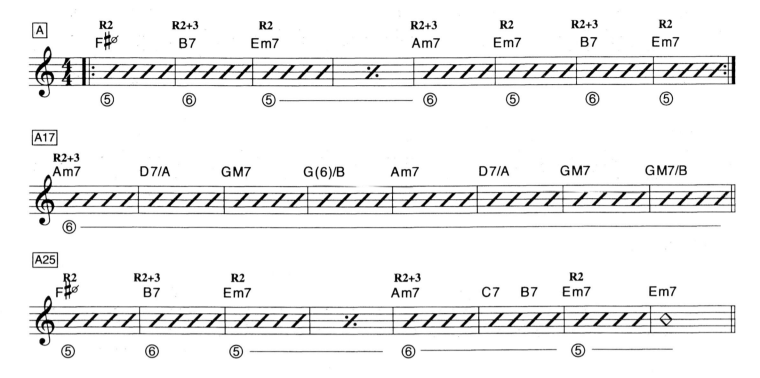

The instructions for which type of voicing has been eliminated on the following exercises. The circled numbers dictate the type of voicing that should be used.

⑥ indicates **R2+3** voicing

⑤ indicates **R2** voicing

Chord Ex. 17

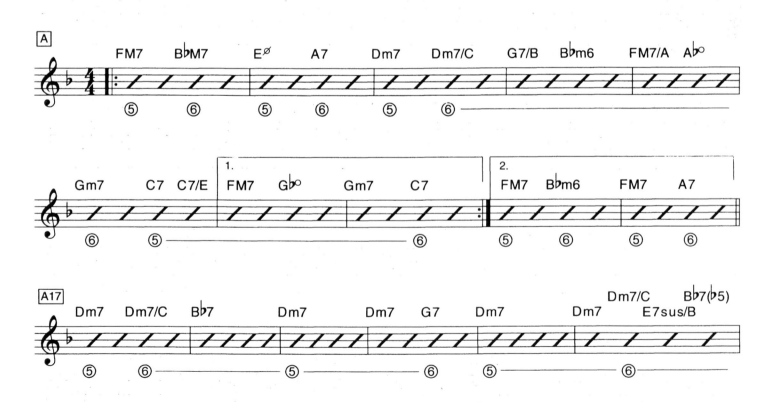

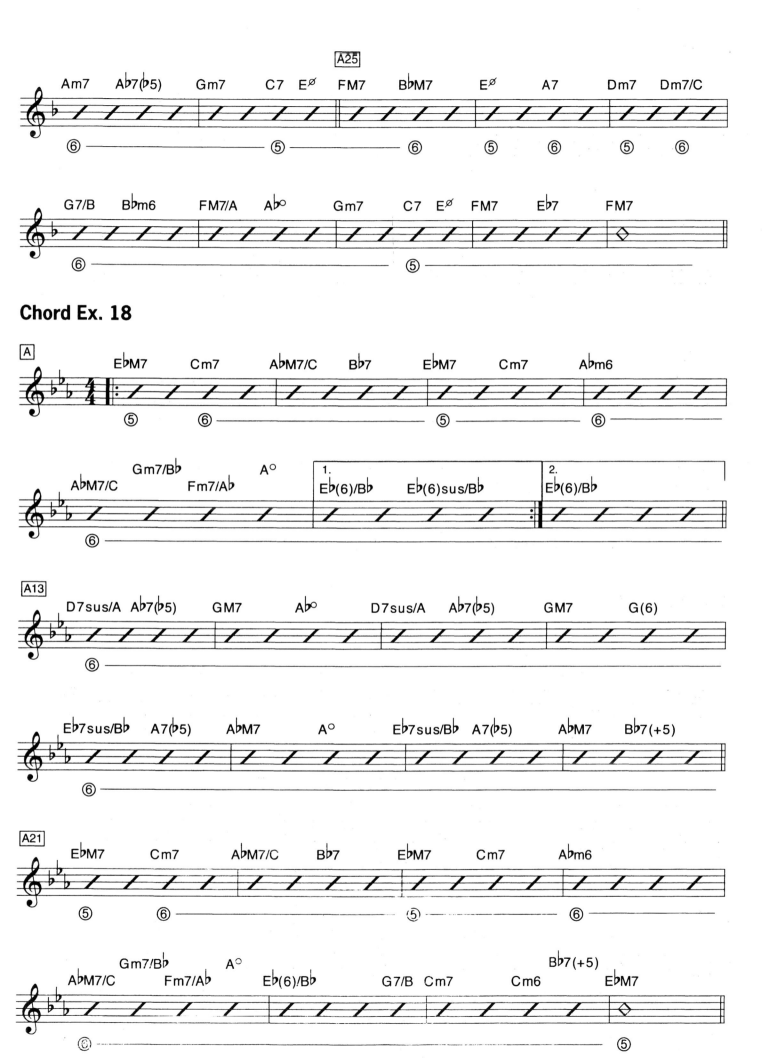

Chord Ex. 18

Chord Ex. 19

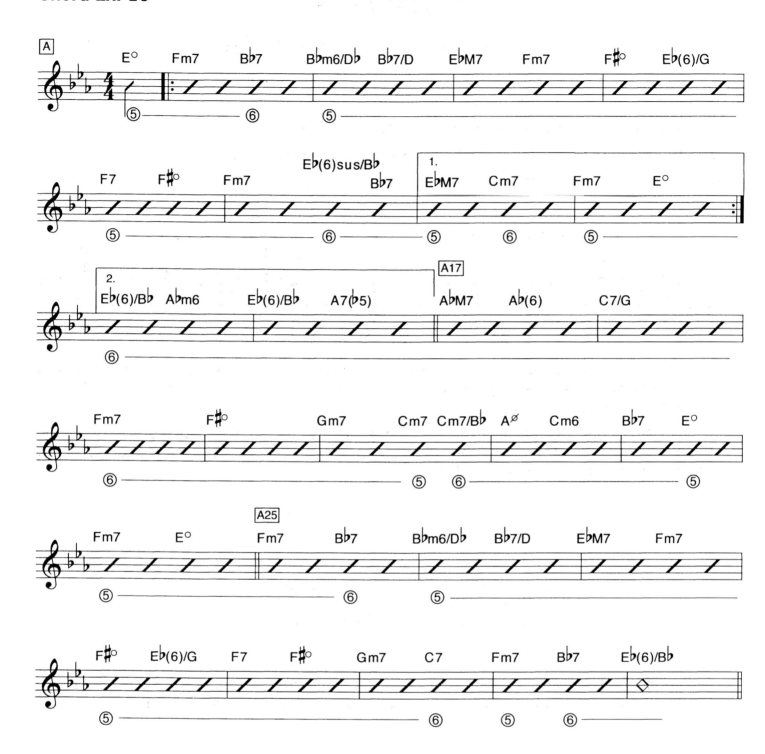

Chapter 4

Ninth, Eleventh, and Thirteenth Chords

When building four-note chords, the basic notes occur in the lower octave such as root, 3rd, 5th, 6th, and 7th. The 9th, 11th, and 13th scale degrees, occur in the upper octave.

(A) The 2nd degree and 9th degree have the same name, but are an octave apart.

(B) The 4th degree and 11th degree have the same name, but are an octave apart.

(C) The 6th degree and 13th degree have the same name, but are an octave apart.

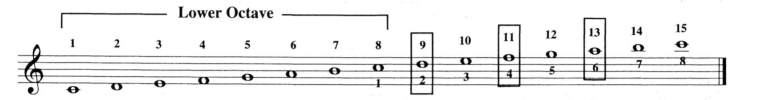

A 9th can be added to any basic major or minor sixth or seventh chords, diminished and half diminished. This two-octave example can occur in any register. Middle C was chosen for this example for convenience in exploring the upper-structure concept.

The 9th can be added to any inversion. The voicings on guitar so far consist of four notes. On any inversion, the 9th should replace the root. Find what string the root is on, and replace the root with 9th on the same string. Arrangers apply this technique when arranging for four horns.

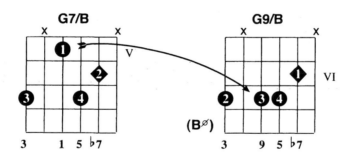

Notice the chord to the right on parenthesis has another name but not the same function. The following illustrates many inversions and how to add the 9th. The inversions are (R2+3) voicings from the 6th string.

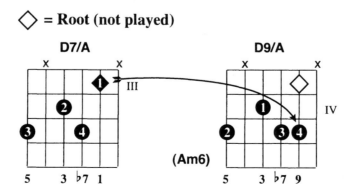

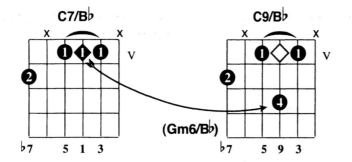

The same procedure applies to the flat nine and sharp nine chords. Add altered 9ths to flat seven chords. Do not add altered 9ths to minor chords. When adding flat 9ths to flat seven chords, there is not a problem. And when adding sharp 9ths, be very careful and use them wisely.

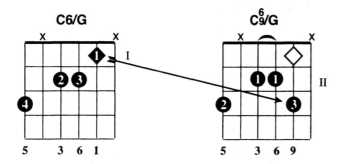

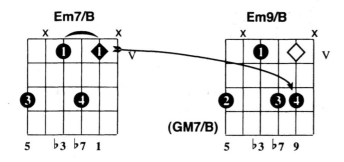

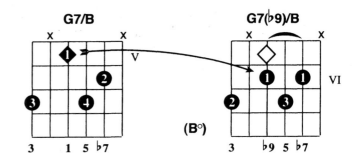

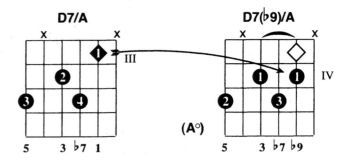

Notice that ♭9 chords and diminished chords are very closely related.

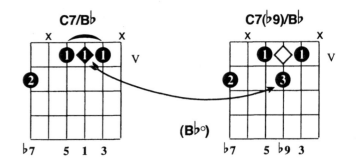

When there is a very dissonant sound, major 3rd and ♯9 are placed closely together. This is because the interval between these two notes is a minor second. These two inversions lend themselves to adding the sharp nines.

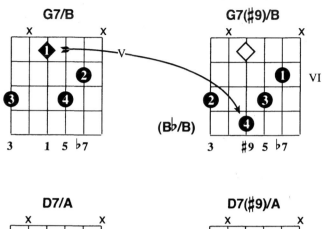

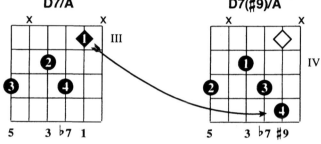

The 13th can replace the 5th of a chord. The distance between 13th and a ♭7th is a half step. This could create a very disonant sound. When the 5th is in bass, do not substitute thirteen in its place. Here are two (R2+3) voicings with 13 and ♭13. Notice that ♭13 and +5 are the same note!

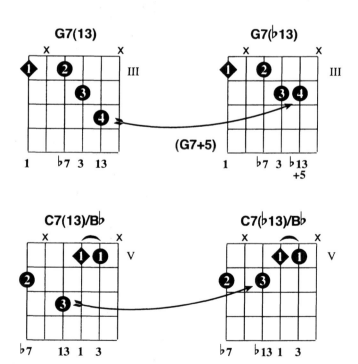

39

Eleventh chords, natural eleven has the same sound as a suspended fourh chord. The inversion with 3rd in bass is omitted with (R2+3) voicings from the 6th string.

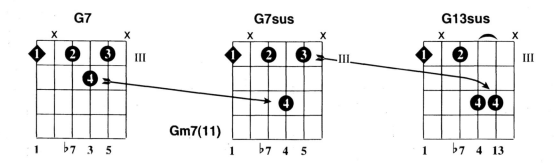

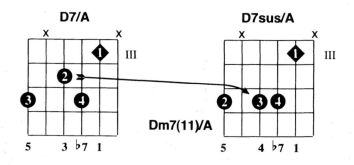

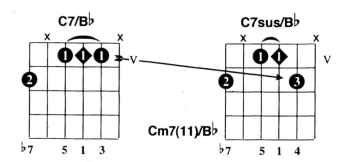

The ♯11 and ♭5 are the same pitch. The ♯11 has a dissonant sound. The ♯11 is not in the diatonic major scale. This means that ♭5 voicings can be substituted for ♯11 chords. Here are two examples with (R2+3) voicings from sixth string.

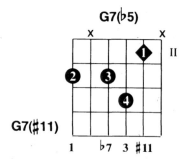

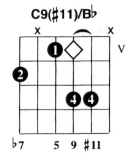

The following charts show how to add the 9th to inversions on the 5th string major or minor (R2) voicings.

The same procedure applies when adding flat nines.

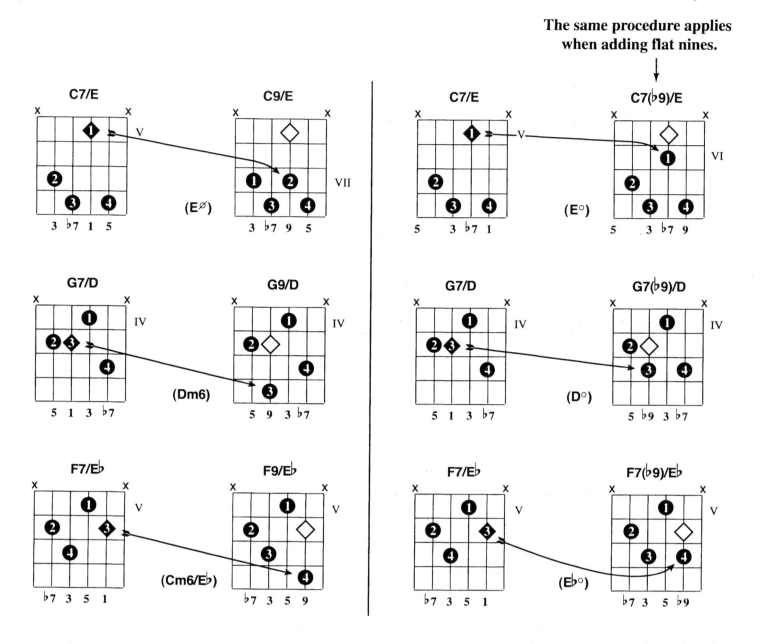

Because of the minor 2nd interval between the major 3rd and #9, here are two (R2) voicings for 7#9 chords.

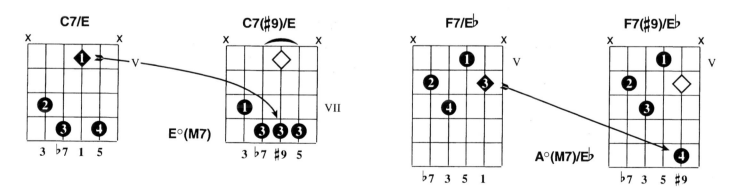

Because the b5 and #11 are the same pitch, b5 voicings can be substituted for chords with a #11. A #11 chord can have a natural 5th within the voicing when adding #11 in place of the 3rd. The 9th has been added to some of these voicings.

Here are (R2) voicings on 5th string.

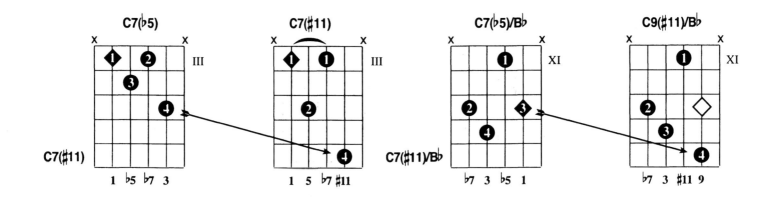

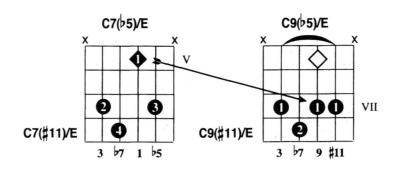

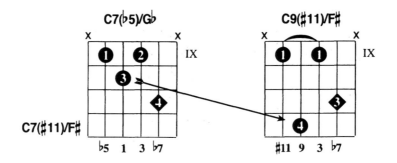

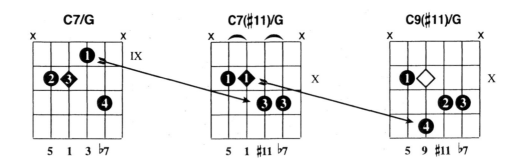

The 13th and 9th can be added to all these voicings. There are more possibilities on the 5th string than the 6th.

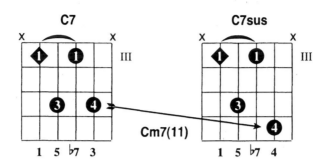

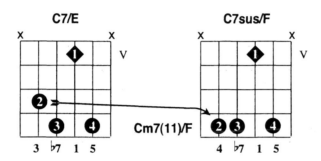

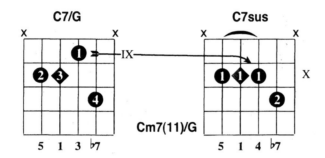

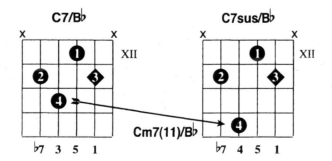

To sum up this chapter, 9, ♭9, ♯9 replaces the root, 11, ♯11 replaces the 3rd, 13, ♭13 replaces the 5th.

There are many possibilities by combining these rules. There is no way of putting every voicing in this book.

Chapter 5

Root Color Tones

Color Tones of chord are the 3rd, 7th, or 6th, depending on type of chord. In a basic chord, such as C7, the two most important notes of this chord are the 3rd and 7th (meaning the 3rd and 7th degrees of the scale). The least important note of a chord is the 5th, unless it becomes altered, such as, $\flat$5th or augmented 5th.

Root Color Tones (RCT) is a way of connecting chords smoothly up and down the neck, moving root to root, and alternating between the 6th and 5th strings. Placement of the Color Tones are important. By analyzing the E minor seven voicing using the open strings, the Color Tones occur on the fourth and third strings (D and G). D is the $\flat$7th and G is the $\flat$3rd of E minor seven. Place the Color Tones on the 4th and 3rd strings and alternate the roots between the 5th and 6th strings.

Symbol for Root Color Tone (RCT) (6th String)

Major Chords

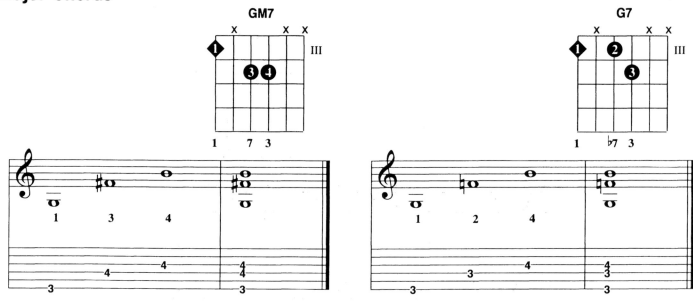

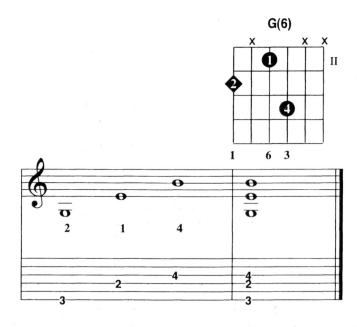

These chords are also refered to as **shell voicings**.

Minor Chords

Gm(M7)

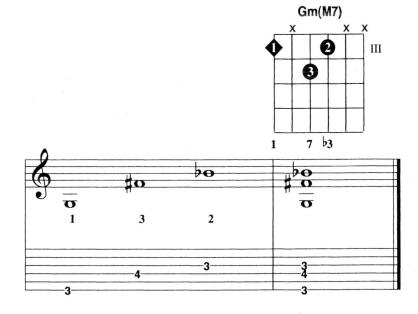

Gm7

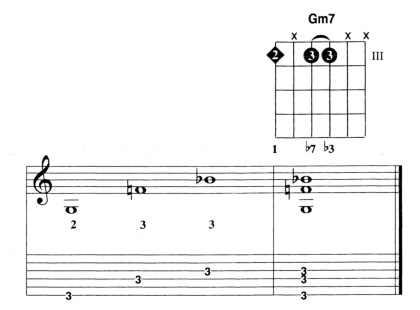

Gm6

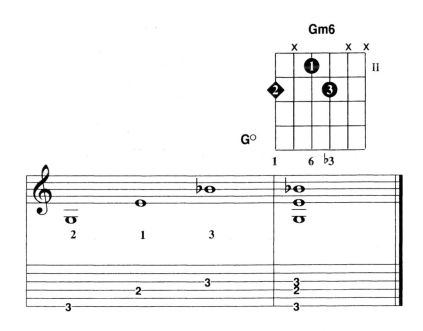

Major Chords

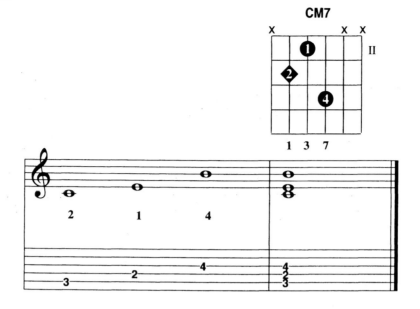

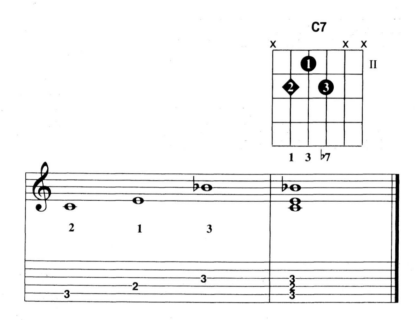

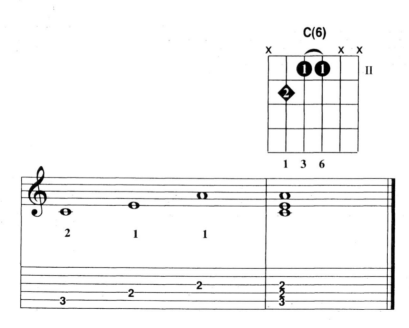

inor Chords

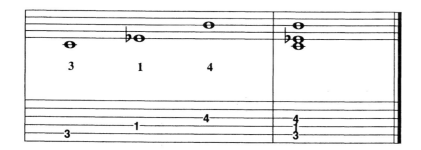

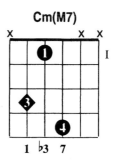

Cm(M7)

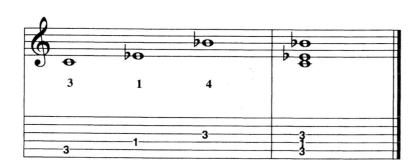

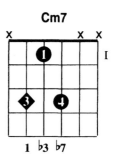

Cm7

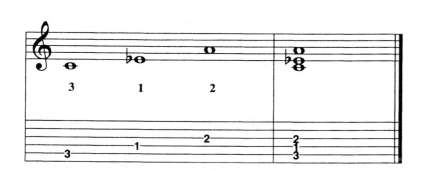

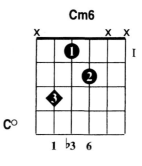

Cm6

C°

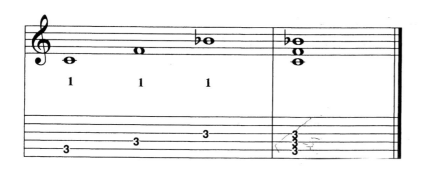

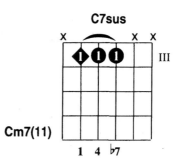

C7sus

Cm7(11)

Use only (RCT) on the following chord progression

Chord Ex. 20

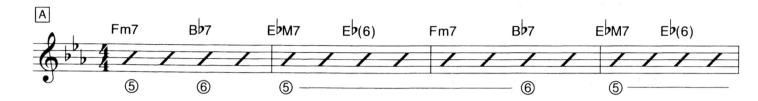

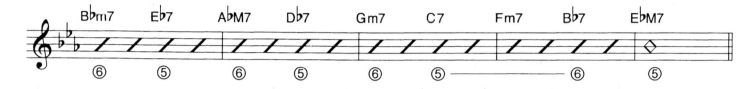

Play the progression again.

(A) Chords based from 6th string, add the 5th on the 2nd string.

(B) Chords based from 5th string, add the 3rd on the 2nd string.

This is called doubleing the 3rd of a chord.

The root or 3rd can be doubled on a chord based from the 5th string except for the major seven chord. There will be a clash between the top two voices. Play the progression again, this time double the root on chords based from the 5th string, except the major seven chord.

This chord progression dictates specific notes to be added on the 2nd string.

Chord Ex. 21

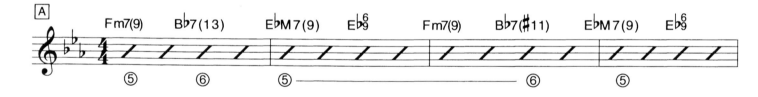

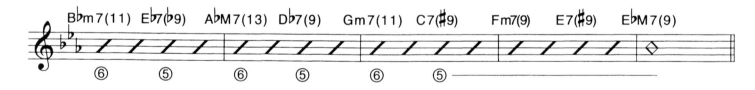

Here are two good guidelines for voicing chords using (RCT)

1. 6th String Voicing

    A. Omit 5th and 1st string

    B. Add 7th or 6th on 4th string

    C. Add 3rd on 3rd string

    D. Add 13th on 2nd String or (5th)

2. 5th String Voicing

  A. Omit 6th and 1st string

  B. Add 3rd on 4th string

  C. Add 7th or 6th on 3rd string

  D. Add root, 9th, or 3rd on the 2nd string

By using all three types of voicings in a chord progression

A. (R2+3) from the 6th string

B. (R2) from the 5th string

C. (RCT) From both the 5th and 6th string.

This will create good continuity and smoothness from one chord to the next.

The next chord progression uses all three types of voicings. The type of voicing will be dictated above the chord symbol and string number will be below the staff.

Chord Ex. 22

For five note voicings, add additional notes on the 1st string!

Chapter 6
Open Triads

Triads based from the 6th string.

Transpose the middle note of a close triad up one octave.

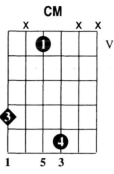

Root Position

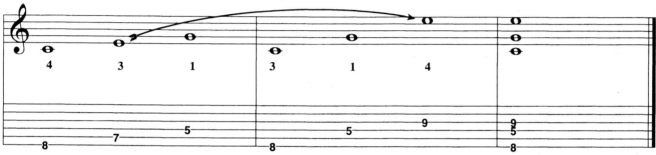

First Inversion

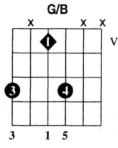

Second Inversion

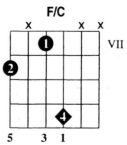

The symbol for Open Triads is (**OT**)

Chord Ex. 23

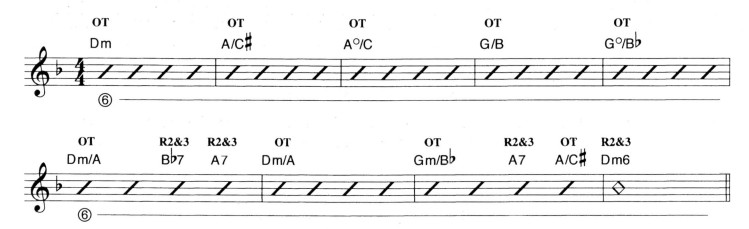

When the **Open Triad** has the root or 3rd in the bass, the middle note can be doubled on the 2nd string one octave higher.

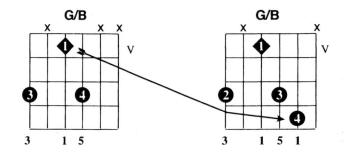

This procedure creates a four note voicing. Redo Ex. 23 with this idea.

Combination of all voicings

R2+3	–	6th String
R2	–	5th String
RCT	–	6th and 5th Strings
OT	–	6th String

Chord Ex. 24

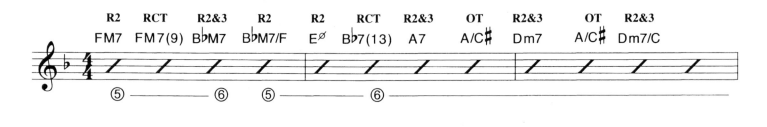

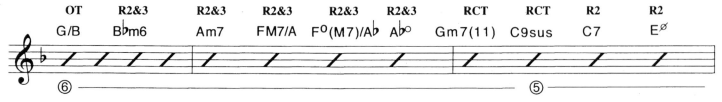

Shell Voicings from the 6th String

Shell Voicings consist of three notes. The Root Color Tones (RCT) is one type of Shell Voicing. To create shell voicings using (R2+3) from the 6th string, omit whichever note occurs on the 2nd string.

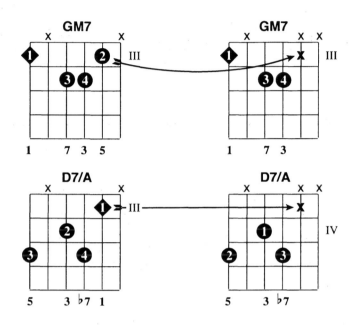

Redo chapter one using this technique on every chord and chord progression.

Shell Voicings from the 5th string (R2)

Omit whichever note occurs on the 4th string.

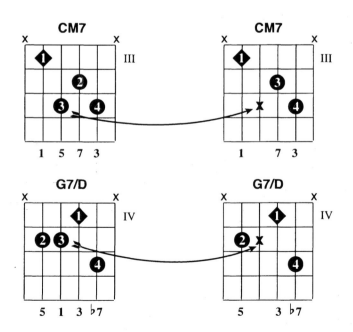

Redo chapter two using this technique on every chord and chord progression.

Chapter 7
Crossovers

Crossover is vertical motion across the neck.

    A.   Move every note in a chord voicing to adjacent string in the same fret.

    B.   Move whichever note used to be located on the 3rd string up one fret to the right.

6th String Crossovers (R2+3)

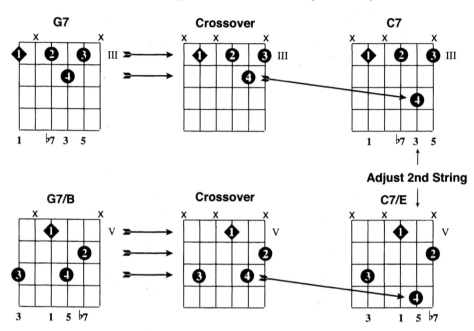

Automatically the chord has been transposed up a perfect 4th.

5th String Crossover

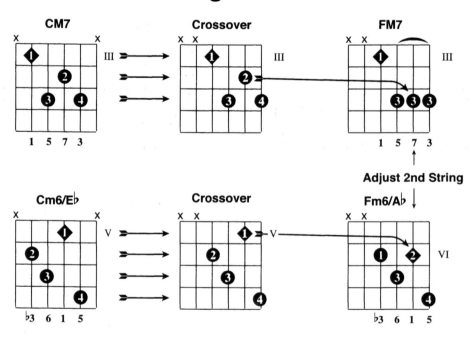

To understand the magnitude of crossovers, redo chapters one through seven. Write out and transpose every chord and chord progression up a perfect 4th, using this technique. This increases chord knowledge 100%.

To reverse Crossovers, lower whichever note occurs on the 3rd string.

Chapter 8
Transfers

Transfers are the transposition of a single note moving one or two octaves from string to string. Moving the note ~~G~~ on the 6th string to the note G on the 1st string. Transposition of G is two octaves, and the transfer is 6 to 1 ~~(6-1)~~. Use only basic chords.

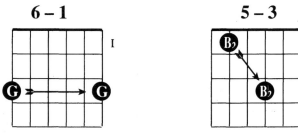

On a transfer, the chord type remains the same, only one note has been changed.

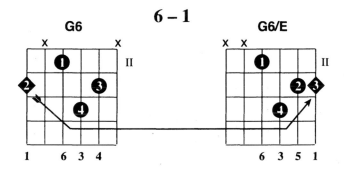

Crossovers transpose the entire chord. Do not get **Crossovers** and **Transfers** confused.

Transfers for 6th String Voicings (R2+3)

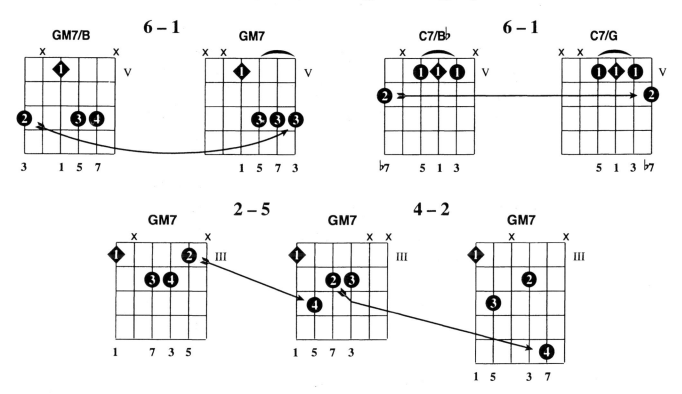

Redo Chapter 1 using these new techniques on every chord.

Transfers for 5th String Voicings (R2)

There can be more than one transfer from the same voicing.

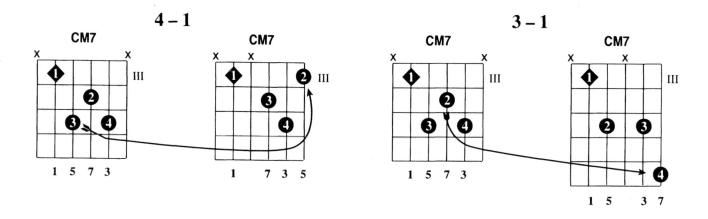

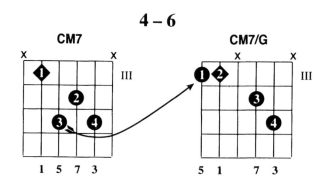

Combining Transfers and Crossovers will create many voicings.

Redo chapter two using these techniques. There are many more transfers that are not in this book.